MEMORY IMPROVEMENT

Train Your Mind To Unlock Your Brain's Potential for a Better Standard of Living

BOOK DESCRIPTION

Memory is no doubt a critical part of our brain without which living life is impossible. We need good memory for studies, work, home activities, and relationships, among other important domains of life.

This book provides you with critical information, hacks and strategies on how to boost your memory so you can achieve greater mental acuity and lead a more productive life.

The guide starts by helping you to understand how memory works. It goes further to explain to you the brain-memory-mind relationship and how this relationship is critical to your memory improvement.

Importance of memory improvement cannot be overlooked. This guide provides scenarios in which memory plays a great role and without which you wouldn't be able to make any successful endeavors, be it in your studies, work, home, relationships or other engagements. It goes further to demonstrate to you how memory improvement relates to your real life so that you can be able to have an above-average understanding of how important memory improvement is to your wellbeing and how you can harness it to boost your mental acuity and lead a more productive life.

You will not be able to deal with forgetfulness and memory loss without understanding its causes, the distinction between forgetfulness, age-related memory loss and dementia. There is that loss which is natural and there is that loss which is actually a medical condition. You need to know the difference so that you can take appropriate remedial action. Yet, even if you get to know the difference, you need to be able carry out self-diagnosis to know the kind of memory loss that you are suffering from so that get to know the best approach to make. This guide provides elaborate information on the types of memory loss, causes, possible tests and diagnosis.

Once you have been able to understand how memory works, causes of memory loss, memory tests and diagnosis, you are now able to think of possible solutions. This guide provides you with practically proven, effective memory hacks and strategies to improve your memory - be it to boost your studies, work, home activities, relationships or otherwise.

Finally, you need to make memory improvement a part of your everyday life. You need to live it. It has to become your lifestlyle. This guide wraps up by recommending to you long-term lifestyle habits to improve your memory so you enjoy perpetual success for as long as you live.

Enjoy reading!

ABOUT THE AUTHOR

George Pain is an entrepreneur, author and business consultant. He specializes in setting up online businesses from scratch, investment income strategies and global mobility solutions. He has built several businesses from the ground up, and is excited to share his knowledge with readers.

DISCLAIMER

Copyright © 2017

All Rights Reserved

No part of this book can be transmitted or reproduced in any form including print, electronic, photocopying, scanning, mechanical or recording without prior written permission from the author.

While the author has taken the utmost effort to ensure the accuracy of the written content, all readers are advised to follow information mentioned herein at their own risk. The author cannot be held responsible for any personal or commercial damage caused by information. All readers are encouraged to seek professional advice when needed.

CONTENTS

MEMORY IMPROVEMENT 1

BOOK DESCRIPTION 2

ABOUT THE AUTHOR 5

DISCLAIMER 6

INTRODUCTION 9

UNDERSTANDING HOW MEMORY WORKS 11

THE BRAIN-MEMORY-MIND RELATIONSHIP 22

IMPORTANCE OF MEMORY IMPROVEMENT 29

HOW MEMORY IMPROVEMENT RELATES TO REAL LIFE ... 33

CAUSES OF FORGETFULLNESS AND MEMORY LOSS 37

MEMORY TESTS AND DIAGNOSIS 43

MEMORY CUES 51

HACKS AND STRATEGIES TO IMPROVE YOUR MEMORY 56

MEMORY ENCODING HACKS AND STRATEGIES 62

MEMORY CONSOLIDATION AND RETENTION HACKS AND STRATEGIES 70

MEMORY RECALL HACKS AND STRATEGIES 74

MEMORY HACKS TO BOOST YOUR STUDIES 79

MEMORY HACKS TO BOOST YOUR WORK 82

MEMORY HACKS TO BOOST YOUR HOME ACTIVITIES 87

MEMORY HACKS TO BOOST YOUR RELATIONSHIPS 92

AGE-RELATED MEMORY HACKS AND STRATEGIES 97

LONG-TERM LIFESTYLE HABITS TO IMPROVE YOUR MEMORY 100

CONCLUSION 106

INTRODUCTION

What would life be like without memory? No studies, no work, no relationships, no life! How else would you have a life if you cannot enjoy it? The joys of life come from reliving memories of the great moments of life - those moments that you were at your best.

Knowledge exists because there is memory to store it. You learn because of experience. Experience is a memory of what you went through at certain moments in the past. Relationships are built based on knowledge and experience. Love is based on relationships. Without knowledge, without experience, without love, how would the world look like? Would you even know that the world exists?

More than anything else, without memory, life will simply not exist. You are a product of genetic memory. Without genetic memory, cells cannot be created. Without cells, your body cannot be formed. Yes, memory is what life is. Simply don't neglect it. It is a whole world of who you are, and what it actually is – MEMORY.

This book provides you with one of the greatest secrets of life – how to improve your memory. It has proven practical hacks and strategies on how to boost your memory to achieve greater mental acuity and lead a more productive life.

Keep reading!

Thank you.

UNDERSTANDING HOW MEMORY WORKS

What is memory?

To understand what memory is, we have to look at it from the various perspectives that define it. All these perspectives help us to gain an in-depth understanding of memory in order to improve it in the most optimal way. It must be noted that each of these perspectives is not a substitute to the other but complementary. It is like looking at an object from different angles in order to understand its various dimensions so that you are able to get its true picture.

We have two broad perspectives of memory;

- The ordinary literal perspective
- The scientific perspective

Ordinary literal perspective

In our day-to-day literal perspective, memory is simply the aggregate total of that which we can remember.

Scientific perspective

Memory has different definitions and interpretations depending on the various scientific perspectives. We have two main scientific perspectives regarding memory;

1. Neurological perspective
2. Psychological perspective

Neurological perspective on memory

The neurological perspective looks at memory as an organic part of the brain. Thus, it is a physiological, or rather, biological perspective of memory.

In this neurological perspective, memory is simply a set of encoded neurons in the brain.

Psychological perspective on memory

In the psychological perspective of memory, memory is human's ability to encode, store, retain and subsequently retrieve information of past experiences in the brain.

This perspective focuses less on the biological nature and function of the memory and more on the psychological nature and function of the memory. There is less emphasis on the biomechanics of encoding, storage and retrieval but more emphasis on the utility of the memory and its effects.

The emphasis is heavily in favor of the nature of the information stored rather than the storage tank itself. Psychology looks at the impact on certain stored information on behavioral characteristics such as joy, happiness, satisfaction, anger, sadness, stress, trauma, depression, among other behavioral attributes. It is in these considerations that mind becomes a critical factor. Thus, in this perspective, the desire to rewire the brain so as to avoid negative behaviors becomes necessary.

Where is memory located?

Memory is a complex web comprising of interconnected nodes via threads. You can't just find memory in one part of the brain as you would do of books in a library or of a memory chip in a computer. Thus, memory is a distributed network of nodes in the brain. Various nodes are found in different parts of the brain. It is an intricate web like the internet with each node representing a server of some sort.

The interplay of the various parts of memory – the ridding bicycle example

For example, taking a simple task as riding a bicycle, there are various parts of memory nodes involved.

- There is that part of the memory involved in recalling how to operate a bicycle - climb on the bike, balancing your body out on the bicycle and pushing the pedals to ride while directing the front wheel using handlebars.
- There is that part of memory involved in recalling how to navigate the various paths and blocks.
- There is that part memory involved in recalling the rules of the road including keeping on one side of the road, dangers of an incoming car and how you ought to behave.
- And then, there is that part of the memory that recalls what you ought to do when tire bursts or hit a pavement wall or a sudden bump.

Thus, memory is not located at one central place in the brain.

How is memory formed?

Memory is formed through four critical stages;

- Encoding
- Consolidation
- Storage
- Retrieval

Encoding

Encoding refers to the conversion of the perceived information into a form that can be stored.

Consolidation

Consolidation, in most cases, is not considered as an independent stage but rather a process. It is a transient stage between encoding and storage where similar codes are put together for effective storage or encoding. For example, bits of information can be quickly encoded, temporarily stored in the short-term memory awaiting more bits so that a reasonable chunk can be encoded and an appropriate cue assigned for further storage into the long-term memory.

Thus, in simple sense, consolidation is the process by which short-term memory is converted into long-term memory. However, consolidation plays a major role other than just codifying or bringing together various bits of information. It is actually the sanitizing process of memory.

In this sanitization, consolidation acts on the memory in such a manner like what we know in computer disk maintenance as "error checks", "defragmentation" and "optimization". It is in the optimization of the memory that consolidation serves to update and improve the memory by adding more clarity to it. For example, when you tell a story or you teach people, you realize that there are certain gaps in your knowledge or some points that are not clear enough. In order for your audience to understand better, you establish newer facts, better terminology, or good examples to make your points understood. Yes, you glue up the various pieces of information together to form a coherent whole. As you do these, consolidation process updates your memory. Thus, it retrieves, re-encodes it and stores it again. So, you will find that the next time you tell the same story or teach the same topic, the information provided will be much more compact, easily delivered and much more understandable.

It goes without saying that, in this regard, and as we shall see later, the largest part of memory improvement takes part during the consolidation process.

Storage (retention)

This is refers to the process of keeping encoded information in a form that can last and be retrievable. Memory storage is sometimes referred to memory retention.

Retrieval (recall)

Retrieval or recall is the process of getting specific information stored and decoding it so that it can be utilized for the needs of the moment. Retrieval is also referred to as recall.

What are the different types of memory?

It is important to understand the different types of memory. This way, when we engage in the process of memory improvement we understand what is happening and how we can better achieve our goals.

Memory is in various forms. These forms are classified based on;

- Duration
- Accessibility

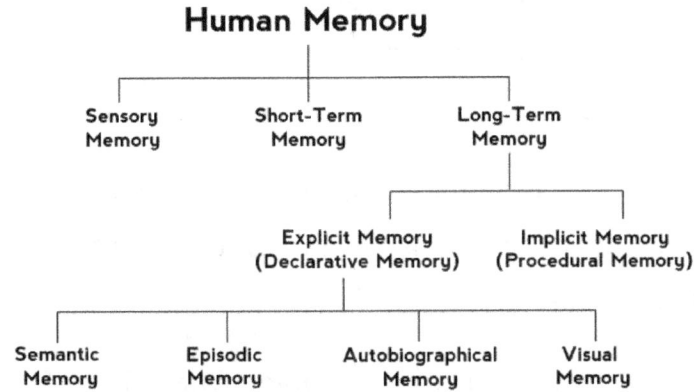

Classification based on duration

Based on duration, we do have three types of memory;

1. Instant (sensory) memory
2. Short-term memory
3. Long-term memory

Instant (sensory) memory

This is a memory that is focused on retaining the impression of a sensory information/signal after the original stimuli (source) has ended. It acts as buffer storage for the information received from the five senses;

- Sight – iconic memory
- Hearing – echoic memory
- Smell – olfactory memory
- Touch – hepatic memory
- Taste – gustatory memory

Of all the five senses and their respective memories, olfactory memory is the most enduring and thus it lasts several times longer than others.

Sensory memory can be either ignored or perceived. For example when you are walking around the field, there are so many things that your eyes see e.g. grass, trees, among others. But, most of them are ignored since you have been seeing them daily. However, if you happen to see a giraffe in that field, it is such rare thing (unless in a zoo or park). Thus, you are more likely to perceive it and store its information due to its **distinctiveness**. The same applies to people that we interact with on daily basis. You will take a small fraction of a second to flash and scan the image of a known person. Unless there is something unique on the person or you desire to engage that person, that image will be ignored almost as fast as it came.

Typically, sensory memory lasts between 200ms to 500ms. The only exception is the olfactory memory that could spread into the domain of the short-term memory.

Short term memory

This is a memory that lasts in the range of a few seconds. It is commonly known as working memory. It is in this working memory that the conscious mind actively wonders, thus bringing about movement of thoughts. The subconscious mind operates within the domain of the long-term memory.

Long term memory

This memory lasts for as long as lifetime. Long-term memory is further divided into two broad categories depending on accessibility;

- Explicit
- Implicit

Explicit memory (conscious memory)

This is memory where you must specifically (consciously) recall it in order to access it. It is called declarative memory since you must declare its specific attributes for it to come about.

The explicit memory is used for encoding, storage and retrieval of facts and events.

The explicit memory is further divided into three types;

- Episodic memory
- Semantic memory
- Autobiographic memory

Episodic memory

This is memory relates to encoding, storage and retrieval of explicit descriptions of actual events (episodes). It is a recollection memory that retains highly detailed sensory perception knowledge.

Semantic memory

This memory relates to encoding, storage and retrieval of meaning and knowledge gained from experiences (including episodes)

Autobiographic memory

Autobiographic memory is generally a hybrid combination of both episodic memory and semantic memory. It doesn't have full recollection as episodic memory, it provides context (semantic) that can instantiate episodic memory. Thus, it is a semantic component that triggers the episodic component.

Implicit memory (unconscious memory)

This is a memory which you need not specifically recall it. It comes almost spontaneously (unconsciously) on its own. It is instinctive by nature.

The implicit memory is used for encoding, storage and retrieval of procedural or routine tasks and skills.

This is the memory that you employ when you are driving, eating, walking, running, among other routine work. It allows activities to be rendered in an almost automatic mode. This memory makes our daily repetitive activities much easier to undertake thus relieving our 'thinking' brain to focus on non-routine activities.

The more you are able to code repetitive tasks into the implicit memory, the lighter your daily activities become and the less your brain gets overworked.

THE BRAIN-MEMORY-MIND RELATIONSHIP

The brain-memory-mind relationship is such a complex relationship. As we clearly understand that memory is part of the brain, then, the brain-memory relationship is not such a difficult issue to discern. However, the brain-mind relationship has been a hot topic in the neuroscience and other psychology domains. This hot topic is what is commonly referred to as the **brain-mind problem**. The brain-mind problem is so complex that a specialized branch of science known as **cognitive neuropsychology** has been dedicated to its study.

Nonetheless, our intent in this section is not really to dwell into the brain-mind problem but to discuss how this relationship affects memory and subsequently discern how it can be dealt with in such a way as to improve memory.

"Brain power without memory power is like a supersonic jet without a fuel tank"

The relationship between brain and memory is akin to that between a jet and its fuel tank. The fuel tank is a store of energy that is utilized in propelling the jet. Without it, the jet can't exist, leave alone not functioning. It is a part of the jet.

"Brain is the CPU hardware, mind is the software"

The brain-mind relationship is better understood using the computer analogy. Computer hardware needs software to be able to function. Yet, without the hardware, the software has no residence. It simply remains a concept in human mind.

The hardware has memory. It is in this memory that the software finds its residence so as to be able to operate the hardware. It is similar to a jet and the pilot. The jet has an engine (the brain) a pilot's cabin (the memory) and the mind (the pilot). Without the pilot's cabin, the pilot has no residence on the jet. Without a residency, the pilot cannot control the jet engine that propels the jet.

So, what is mind?

Mind is a set of cognitive faculties responsible for manifestation of thought, perception, emotion, determination, memory and imagination that takes place within the brain. It is the thought process of reasoning. It is consciousness we know, the ability to control what we do, and know what we are doing and why. It is responsible for processing of feelings and emotions, resulting in attitudes and actions.

How does mind affect the memory and brain?

As we shall see later, just as software is used to write and store programs in the computer memory, the mind can be used to write and store 'programs' or codes into the human memory. These programs or codes are what we know as mindset.

It is the mindset that directs our thought process and determines our attitudes and behaviors. It is the mindset that directs our conscious actions.

Human memory is highly flexible. It is like a balloon. It can expand and can contract, within certain limits. To achieve higher memory capacity it needs practice. We have to develop habits that seek to expand this memory. It is like our lungs. If you want to expand the capacity of your lungs, you have to cultivate a habit of making deep inhalations and exhalations. Most of the time, we underutilize our lungs by cultivating a habit of making shallow inhalations and exhalations. There are many negative health effects of this. We are not going to dwell into that. But, we must also realize that the same applies to our memory.

If we often underutilize our memory by not effectively utilizing its already available capacity, it is not likely going to grow and expand. This limits the extent of our capacity to effectively function as human beings. It is just like having a computer memory card. You can't buy a higher capacity memory card if the lower capacity memory card that you have is more than enough for your needs. But, unlike memory card where you will be forced to buy another one, our human memory is such that it is expandable. Thus, we cannot acquire a new or another human memory as a replacement.

The side-effect of a constricted memory capacity is that our brain capacity also becomes constrained. The relationship between memory and brain's processing ability is akin to that of the crushing part of a flour mill and the hopper where grain is poured. If the hopper is small, it simply means less can be poured into it at a time. This also means less can be fed into the crusher. However fast the crusher is, or powerful the motor is, if the capacity of the hopper is small, the output of corn mill won't increase. The inverse is the same. In this analogy, simply take the hopper as your memory and the crusher as your brain. The ability of your brain to deliver output (information) will depend on the capacity of your memory (data and instructions).

In a computer, there are several 'memory nodes' each with a specific function. For example, the hard disk is a memory. It stores both the Operating Software and the Application software plus the bulk of data. There is also the RAM (Random Access Memory). This is closest to the CPU (Central Processing Unit) which is akin to our brain. Within the CPU, we do have Memory Cache (extremely short memory).

Using the Computer memory analogy, our sensory memory is like Memory Cache; our Working Memory is akin to RAM and our Long-term Memory is similar to Hard Disk.

As seen earlier, our mindset is akin to software. Yet, the computer has two sets of software, the Operating Software (OS) and the Application Software (AS). Using the same analogy, the OS represents our Unconscious mindset (in the long-term memory) and the AS represents our Conscious mindset (in the short-term memory). We know both the OS and the AS resides in the hard-disk. So, it is more about the functions of these software (mindsets) rather than where they are stored that differentiates them.

Our short-term memory is our working memory. It is where instructions (conscious mindset) and data relating our current (conscious) activity (application) are stored. On the other hand, our long-term memory is unconscious memory. It is where instructions (unconscious mindset) and data relating to our non-current (unconscious) activity are stored. The unconscious activity is reflex activity that we don't have to explicitly call to action.

In computer, the software instructs the CPU on what to do (what to process). Similarly, our mindset instructs our brain on how to process certain inputs (data or signals from external stimuli) so as to give desired output. Thus, if we can rewire (reprogram) our mindset (just as we can reprogram Computer software) we can also rewire (reprogram) how our brain processes inputs.

Another thing that we learn from the computer analogy is that the software determines the timing, the order of priority and the nature of data to be fed into the working memory so that the brain can process it. In this regard, the mindset or the mind at large, determines how we utilize our memory. This is very important, and worth emphasis: **The mind determines how we utilize our memory**.

When you buy a new computer, its memory is never completely empty. Neither is it completely empty of software. There is minimal memory and software required to enable starting up, managing basic computer resources and shutting of the computer. This is done by the manufacturer and the computer user has no control over it. This memory and software is stored in what we call BIOS (Basic Input and Output System). Without BIOS the computer cannot start, the keyboard, mouse and screen cannot work. If these can't work, you cannot even install other software on it.

Just as the computer comes with BIOS, we human beings are born with certain memory and mindset. They are stored in our genes. Genes are our kind of BIOS. Thus, how to breath, open and shut eyes and a few other things an infant does immediately when he/she is born already exist as part of the genetic information and instructions stored in our genetic memory. This enables the infant to survive. Neither the mother nor the infant has control over these. This genetic information and instructions have been coded since the existence of the human species and continues to be consolidated without human's conscious intervention. This is what is needed for a human's bare survival on earth. Non-genetic information and instructions are acquired through learning and experience.

In this book, we won't focus on the genetic memory as this is beyond our scope. It is good to know that genetic memory exists. But, our focus is going to be on that which is consciously within our control. We can only deliberately improve the memory that we can consciously alter how we use it.

IMPORTANCE OF MEMORY IMPROVEMENT

Why it is important to cultivate good memory? Why is memory so important?

The importance of memory cannot be overlooked. First of all, memory is part of the brain. The brain can't exist without it. Without memory I couldn't even write what you are reading. Neither could you read and comprehend what I have written. Thus, memory is important not just for our comprehension but also our communication and interactions. Thus, it is so natural that improving memory will boost our overall well-being in all our faculties and domains of our existence.

We can briefly highlight some of the importance of improved memory to our wellbeing.

- **Improved cognition** – Cognition is our ability to perceive and recognize stimuli, be it internal or external. Without cognition, we are brain-dead. Improvement in cognition boosts our other faculties of life.

- **Improved intuition** – Our intuition is based on our unconscious memory. Without our unconscious memory, it would be difficult for us to carry out routine tasks as basic as biting, chewing and swallowing food. It would be difficult to even breathe. With improved intuition, we advance beyond the normal basic routing to be able to almost by reflex detect things and act upon them. This is important if we have to escape from danger. People with supernormal degree of intuition are the ones we commonly refer to as geniuses, prophets, seers and the like.

- **Improved communication** – Communication depends on our interpretation of the signals which we perceive. These signals are compared to information stored in our memory, processed and an appropriate feedback given as response. With improved memory, the knowledge tank becomes bigger and thus we can store more references in our memory for advanced communication.

- **Improved understanding** – When we are better able to effectively communicate, our understanding goes up. This is because we are able to properly perceive signals, synthesize them, and interpret them.

- **Improved relationships** – Relationships are all about communication and understanding. With improved communication and understanding, it is obvious that our relationships are more likely going to improve.

- **Improved academic performance** – Improved cognition, intuition, communication and understanding leads to improved academic performance.

- **Improved sports and fitness performance** – Learning a new sport and new fitness patterns or perfecting them requires good memory. With improved cognition and intuition, mastering these patterns and boosting reflex responses increases our sports and fitness performance.

- **Improved quality of leisure** – Leisure is about being able to relax and use your time for pleasurable non-routine activities. To learn new non-routine activities, and to enjoy the moments, we need to have good sensory memory. The more our sensory memory improves, the more likely we are going to enjoy our leisure activities. To be able to recall these pleasurable moments later on so that we can continue being inspired requires our ability have great autobiographic and episodic memory.

- **Improved appreciation of nature** – Nature is all there is that has ever been. Our advancement depends on how we are able to appreciate nature. This appreciation comes from accumulating knowledge of the various facts about nature. We have biology that focuses on the nature of living things, physics that focuses on the non-biological nature and chemistry that focuses on core elements of matter. These are diverse subjects. The more you are able have knowledge of them (stored information about them), the more likely you are able to appreciate nature.

- **Improved lifestyle** – Lifestyle improves the moment we are able to appreciate the nature of things and the nature of beings. It is through this appreciation that we are able to achieve balance and harmony with our nature.

HOW MEMORY IMPROVEMENT RELATES TO REAL LIFE

A lot of times, things happen in such unconscious ways such that we even 'forget' that we do have memory. It is when we try to recall something that we come into consciousness about the existence of our memory.

First of all, how to we come to realize 'real life'? How do we come to distinguish it from 'non-real' life? How do we even identify life as 'unreal'? What is that which is 'unreal'?

In an attempt to answer these questions, we will come to the conclusion that the difference between the 'real' and 'unreal' is determined by our own memory.

That which is 'real' is what we have knowledge of and proven its existence. It is a fact of existence. On the other hand, that which is 'unreal' we have no knowledge of it. Consequently, we lack basis to prove its existence. Imaginations, dreams, fantasies, and beliefs are part of the unreal.

What we have to keep on reminding ourselves is that knowledge is memory. This is very fundamental.

To be able to understand how memory improvement relates to real life, let's consider a scenario in which our memory could only store data and instructions for only five minutes.

The 5-Minutes Memory

Let's apply the 5-minute memory scenario to our real life and just fathom what would be our daily life if we just had a 5-minute memory.

Study

- Think of how memory helps to store lessons in class – how would you remember what the teacher taught if you had just a 5-minutes long memory? By the time the teacher ends the lesson you would have forgotten almost all that you were taught.
- Think of how memory is key to passing exams – how would you master complex mathematical formulas and rightly apply them to exams that would come more than 5 minutes later? You simply won't have any answer to give.

Work

- Would you get to your workplace if you only had a 5-minutes memory?
- Would you remember tasks assigned to you by supervisor?

- Would you remember what you learned about how to do it?

You simply won't be able to do the normal kind of work that we do on day-to-day basis.

Relationships

- Think about how a baby memorizes its mother and shoots a self-defense mechanism against strangers
- Think of how good memories of dating and wedding helps to keep the marriage glue from disintegrating
- Think about past memories of dating, love and romance

Would you really be able to have these if you had a -5-minute worth of memory? Definitely not. It is practically impossible to have a long-term relationship that can only last 5 or less minutes.

Happiness

- Would you surely be happy if you can't remember your accomplishments and celebrations?
- Would you be happy if you can't remember your loved ones, more so, you husband/wife, son/daughter?

A 5-minute long memory would present probably the unhappiest kind of life.

Daily life

- Would you remember to eat?
- Would you remember where your food is?
- Would you remember to differentiate between salt and sugar and where to put each?
- Would you remember to keep off from poison you had the other moment and wash off your hands?

All these won't be possible. The answer is simply No!

Longevity

- Would you plan for your future?
- Would you remember where your savings are?
- Would you know where to invest?

A memory that lasts only 5 minutes wouldn't enable you to do all these.

CAUSES OF FORGETFULLNESS AND MEMORY LOSS

The desire for memory improvement almost all the times emanate from our forgetfulness. Forgetfulness is in somewhat a memory loss. However, it is natural. Thus, memory loss is more restricted to a much more severe situation. Nonetheless, the difference is largely dependent on the degree to which we can't recall things.

To be able to understand how to improve our memory, it is imperative that we understand some of the causes that may lead to forgetfulness and memory loss.

The causes of memory loss fall into three broad categories;
1. Lifestyle causes
2. Medical conditions
3. Environmental pollution
4. Ageing

Causes due to our lifestyle

Poor lifestyle can have serious effects on our memory thus affecting memory retention and recalling.

The following are the most common lifestyle causes of memory loss;

- Stress and depression
- Trauma
- Poor diet – A diet rich in cholesterol and sugar; poor in vitamins (B-2) and essential minerals, protein deficiency, etc.
- Alcoholism and substance abuse (more so, nicotine abuse)
- Sleep deprivation
- Dehydration – Brain is made up of 80% of water. Losing just 20% of it will cause you start experiencing symptoms of dementia while you don't have it. It is pretty severe. Doing extreme and strenuous physical activity for long hours that make you sweat profusely can cause dehydration and memory loss. This is commonly observed in those who undertake sprints, middle races and even marathons. They lose memory for a while at the end of their races before regaining it moments later during resting.

Causes due to medical conditions

The following are the most common medical conditions that causes memory loss;

- Tumor/clot
- Organ problem – thyroid, kidney or liver
- Infections e.g. neuro-syphilis
- Dementia
- Stroke
- Sleep apnea
- Concussion
- Low blood sugar
- Verterbrobasilar circulatory disorder
- Parkinson's disease
- Seizures
- Hypercalcemia
- Encephalitis
- Neurofibromatosis
- Delirium
- Neurocognitive disorders
- Epilepsy
- Focal onset seizures
- Night terrors
- Whipple's disease
- Multiple sclerosis
- Huntington's disease

- Wernicke Kosserkoff Syndrome
- Tay-Sachs Disease
- Encephalopathy
- Adverse response to medication e.g. antidepressants, antihistamines, some painkillers, sleeping pills, tranquilizers, muscle relaxants, pain medication, cholesterol lowering medication, diabetes medication (e.g. metformin).

Causes due to environmental pollution

Pollution has adverse effects on the memory. It affects all stages and processes of memory.

The following are some of the pollutions that affect memory;

- Noise pollution – This affects encoding, consolidation, retention and recall.

- Water pollution – Industrial and sewer discharge into water sources can cause lead and mercury poisoning. Lead and mercury poisoning have been associated with brain damage and memory loss.

- Air pollution – Studies have found out that dirty particles in the air can lead to inflammation in the respiratory system which spreads out to the rest of the body. This inflammation has been found to trigger or aggravate obesity, diabetes, and high blood pressure. These three medical conditions have been linked to stress, depression and memory loss. Also, heavy metal particles such as lead and mercury particles can be found in air in heavily industrialized zones or cities experiencing heavy petroleum smoke pollution.

- Soil pollution – Heavy metals due to industrial discharge, polluted rainfall, artificial fertilizers, pesticides and herbicides can cause soil pollution. These heavy metals get absorbed by plants that we eat. This eventually enters our digestive system and reaches our nervous system into the brain.

Causes due to ageing

Ageing is natural. As we age, normal functions of our body goes into gradual decline. Our cognitive function gets affected and it too goes into a gradual decline thus resulting into gradual loss of memory.

However, there is that kind of ageing that is abnormal – premature ageing. We don't age at the same rate. The pace of ageing varies from one person to the next.

Luckily, we can avoid premature ageing and slow down the pace of natural ageing. This, way, we can also slow down memory loss.

MEMORY TESTS AND DIAGNOSIS

Like every doctor knows, you can't confront a disease that you hardly know. A disease manifests itself through its symptoms. The symptoms are not the disease but rather warning signals that the disease has arrived and seized you. Thus, in any curative remedy, you confront the disease instead of the symptoms. Once you confront the disease the symptoms disappear. This is so true of memory.

The most unfortunate thing is that, most of us waste our time and resources confronting various symptoms instead of confronting their root causes – the diseases themselves. It is obviously necessary to confront the discomforting symptoms such as pain and forgetfulness just to relieve yourself from their harsh effect. However, this is never curative. It is simply short-term relief. The bad side of it is that it is likely going to condition your mind to forget confronting the real disease.

When it comes to memory, we can easily employ quick memory improvement hacks just to keep remembering things. This is, in essence, confronting the symptoms. It is great, but, it must not make us overlook the disease – the root cause of our forgetfulness and/or memory loss. We must keep on reminding ourselves that the root cause remains unresolved and we must confront in for better long-term results.

Like in normal diseases, symptoms help us identify the unique disease that we are suffering from. Similarly, to be able to identify the type of memory loss we are suffering from, we need to identify its symptoms so that we can device appropriate remedial action.

Symptoms help us to distinguish between three types of memory loss

1. Normal forgetfulness – this is mainly due to temporary causes
2. Age-related forgetfulness – this is mainly due process of ageing
3. Dementia – this is due to mental disorder

Normal forgetfulness – causes and symptoms

As we have indicated previously, forgetfulness is part of memory loss. However, it is temporary and shallow. Forgetfulness is often a result of not easily reaching the right trigger that can bring forth recall. Thus, it is a problem of recalling and retrieving memory. It is not a problem of memory retention.

Most of the time, when we talk about memory loss, technically, we refer to that long-term and deep loss of memory. This, unlike forgetfulness, it affects all stages and processes of memory, including encoding, consolidation, retention and recall. However, the most affected part is memory retention.

Normal forgetfulness is caused by the following;

1. Transience
2. Absentmindedness
3. Blocking
4. Misattribution
5. Suggestibility
6. Bias
7. Persistence

While we can easily distinguish between forgetfulness from other types of memory loss, the greatest challenge comes when trying to distinguish between normal ageing and dementia.

Differences between normal ageing memory loss and dementia

This is by far the most critical of all differences as it could mean the difference between your life and death. Dementia is a pointer to a very serious condition that needs urgent medical attention.

The following are main situations that can help you to quickly differentiate between dementia and norm aging memory loss;

1. Events and Conversations
2. Names of People
3. Frequency of Forgetting
4. Vocabulary Finding
5. Concerns about your memory
6. Places and Directions
7. Judgment and Decision-making
8. Independence
9. Disruptive Personality Changes
10. Disorientation

Events and conversations

Normal aging: Not being able to remember details of a conversation that took place a year ago

Dementia: Not being able to remember details of recent conversations and events

Names of people

Normal aging: Not being able to remember names of some acquaintances

Dementia: Not being able to remember names of loved ones and close family members

Frequency of forgetting

Normal aging: Forgetting things and events occasionally

Dementia: Forgetting things and events more often

Vocabulary finding

Normal aging: Occasionally having difficulty finding words

Dementia: Frequent pauses and substitutions when finding words

Concerns about your memory

Normal aging: You are worried about your memory but your family members and loved ones are not

Dementia: Your relatives and loved ones are worried about your memory but you are not aware of it.

Places and directions

Normal ageing: May pause to remember directions, but, doesn't get lost in familiar places.

Dementia: Unable to recall directions. Gets lost or disoriented even in familiar places.

Judgment and decision-making

Normal aging: Judgment and decision-making doesn't get impaired.

Dementia: Difficulties making choices; may behave in socially inappropriate ways; shows poor judgment.

Independence

Normal aging: Able to function independently and pursue normal activities

Dementia: Difficulty performing simple tasks such as washing up, paying bills and even dressing appropriately.

Disruption personality changes

Normal aging: No serious disruptive personality changes.

Dementia: Manifests serious disruptive personality changes such as aggression, paranoia and impulsiveness.

Disorientation

This is behavioral expression of a person who appears lost. It can include exasperation and even aggression, especially when someone feels constrained, obstructed or imprisoned.

Normal aging: No disorientation

Dementia: Mild to severe disorientation depending on the degree of dementia

Memory tests

Memory tests are diagnostic tools that enable us to detect whether we are experiencing abnormal forgetfulness or even memory loss due to normal aging or dementia.

Memory tests are classified into various categories. However the following are the most common broad categories;

- Short-term memory tests

- Long-term memory tests
- Autobiographic memory tests
- Episodic memory tests

MEMORY CUES

What are memory Cues

Memory cues are specific identifiers that trigger the retrieval of certain basic information. They can be considered as tags or keys. For example, in a conventional library, a book tag enables one to identify a particular book out of hundreds in a particular shelf. Bookmark is another kind of cue that enables one to access and retrieve certain specific information from a book.

Thus memory cues are identifiers that enable easy recall and retrieval of information from the long-term memory. The brain stores each and every set or packet of information into the long-term memory by associating it with a particular cue.

Memory cues can be classified based on the sense that perceives them e.g. sight, hearing, touch, smell or taste.

Examples of memory cues

Each kind of sensory memory has its own particular cue. The following are the various sensory memories that we discussed earlier;

- Sight – Iconic memory
- Hearing – Echoic memory
- Smell – Olfactory memory
- Touch – Hepatic memory
- Taste – Gustatory memory

Examples of iconic memory cues

Examples of iconic memory cues include;

- Color codes – Electric wire color codes, electronic resistors color codes, etc
- Body language – Sign language, nodding, beckoning, etc.
- Signs and symbols – Directional signs, warning signs, etc.

Examples of echoic memory

Examples of echoic memory cues include;

- Meditation/memorization cues – e.g. mantras, etc
- Warning cues e.g. sirens, alarms, etc
- Reminder cues – e.g. clock alarm, mnemonic clock, etc

Examples of olfactory memory

Examples of olfactory memory cues include:

- Scents – in cooking gas, soaps, detergents, paints, garments, deodorants, air fresheners, etc.
- Aroma – in foods, nectar, honey, etc.

Examples of hepatic memory cues

Examples of hepatic memory cues include:

- Meditation/memorization cues – e.g. mala beads
- Acknowledgement cues – e.g. gat
- Affection cues - e.g. kiss, hug, caress, etc

Examples of gustatory memory cues

Examples of gustatory memory cues include:

- sugary taste and flavors
- salty taste and flavors
- sour taste and flavors
- savory taste and flavors
- bitter taste and flavors

These cues can also fall within another kind of categorization depending on whether they are static, contextual or heuristic;

- State-dependent cues – These are cues are based on a certain prevailing state of consciousness. For example, there are certain things that are said when someone is drunk. While the person is sober, he cannot remember those things. But, when the person gets drunk again, he can vividly remember those things that he said. Thus, drunkenness becomes the state-dependent cue in such cases. Emotional cues are some of the state-dependent cues. For example, it has been known that when someone is sad, he tends to remember bad or negative things such as insults, childhood abuses, spousal abuses, etc. However, when the same person is in happy mood, the person remembers good or positive things such as birthday celebrations, wedding anniversary, graduation ceremony, party events, etc.
- Context-dependent cues – These are cues that are based on a particular context. Thus, recalling happens when the context that prevailed during encoding presents itself during recall.
- Heuristic cue – Heuristic cue is that cue that triggers you to apply "a rule of thumb" approach. That is, it triggers you to apply a simple methodological approach to dealing with a certain issue being reminded. For example, a siren is a

heuristic cue that can trigger fire fighters to implement certain fire-fighting procedures. It can trigger the military to engage procedures necessary for high alert. It can also trigger an emergency casualty unit in a hospital to prepare for life saving procedures.

As we will discuss later under memory hacks, we can improve our memory by simply learning to associate memorable cues with the kind of information that we wish to store in our long-term memory.

HACKS AND STRATEGIES TO IMPROVE YOUR MEMORY

We have seen the benefits of improving your memory in our previous sections. We also saw that memory can improved through a proper mindset.

In this section we are going to explore various hacks and strategies you can perform to boost your memory. This will set up the pace for our subsequent sections each of which will deal with specific hacks and strategies in certain domains of our life such as studies, work, home activities, relationships fitness, sports and leisure.

Difference between hacks and strategies

Hacks are quick tactical solutions. Strategies are gradual long-term solutions. Hacks seek to remedy the symptoms by making them less severe while strategies aim at dealing with the root cause. Both are needed and are complementary.

Most hacks to improve memory falls into two broad categories;

- Physiological hacks
- Mental hacks

These hacks must complement each other if a wholesome memory improvement has to be achieved. Choosing one to the exclusion of the other will not optimize memory improvement.

Physiological hacks

Physiological hacks are those hacks that relate to altering the brain's biomechanical process so as to improve memory. These are majorly lifestyle hacks.

These hacks fall into the following categories;

- Detoxification
- Diet
- Fitness workouts

Mind (mental) hacks

Mind hacks are so many and varied. This is because their direct impact on how we behave can be psychologically determined.

Mental hacks fall into the following broad categories;

1. Encoding hacks
2. Consolidation and retention hacks
3. Recalling hacks

Encoding hacks

The following are the most common encoding hacks;

1. Mental games and workouts – including cue recalls
2. Neuroplasticity
3. Neurolinguistic programming
4. Mantra meditation
5. Chunking

Mental games and workouts

Mental games and workouts are those hacks that intent to boost your mind's focus and concentration. Apart from the mind, they help to improve encoding and consolidation, retention (storage) and retrieval. We shall discuss in subsequent sections on the kind of mental games and workouts for each specific area of our life including studies, work, home activity, relationship fitness, sports and leisure.

Neuroplasticity

As we discussed in the section under brain-memory-mind relationship, we found out that it is possible to reprogram our mindset and thus rewire our brain. This act of rewiring the brain is what is known as neuroplasticity. The subject of neuroplasticity is much more complex than this. Thus, it is beyond the scope of this book. Notheneless, you are highly encouraged to gather more information on it from other sources so as to advance your knowledge on how you can improve your memory through neuroplasticity.

Neurolinguistic Programming (NLP)

NLP is another great technique which we can use to remap our mindset so that we can enforce cues and better utilize our mind and memory. Simplistically, NLP is a special technique of using cues to rewire the brain. NLP subject is much more complex than this. Thus, it is beyond the scope of this book. Notheneless, you are highly encouraged to gather more information on it from other sources so as to advance your knowledge on how you can improve your memory through neuroplasticity.

Meditation

Meditation is one of the most effective methods of improving memory and mental acuity. This deserves a section of its own. However, in this section we can mention two widely applied meditation techniques that boost encoding, consolidation, retention and retrieval.

These techniques are;

1. Mantra meditation technique – This is a technique that enables one to encode, consolidate and retrieve memory by use of mantra. Mantra refers repetitive utterances that are made as daily routines. Buddhism, Catholicism and Islam are religions that widely use mantra. Thus, auditory (echoic) cues are used. Indeed, a mantra is simply an auditory cue.

2. Mala meditation technique – This is a technique that uses mala beads for purposes of meditation. Again, Buddhism, Catholicism and Islam use mala beads in their religious activities. Catholics and Muslims use beads (rosary beads in Catholicism) to enact and enchant prayers. Buddhists (from where the word originated) use mala beads for various functions. Some Buddhists use mala beads just as Catholics and Muslims do. Others use mala beads to help focus the mind and thus stop it from wandering.

Chunking

This refers to encoding elements in chunks in the short memory. Short memory is capable of storing between 5 and 9 elements. To store more elements, such as 12 digits, you break them into memorable chunks so that they become fewer units (e.g. 4 or 5 units/chunks)

Recalling hacks

The following are the most common recalling hacks;
1. Memory reminders
2. Mantra
3. Mala

Memory reminders

- Alarm clocks
- Calendars
- Diaries
- Journals
- Signs and symbols

Subsequent sections will dwell deeper into specific memory hacks and strategies.

MEMORY ENCODING HACKS AND STRATEGIES

Memory encoding hacks and strategies are those that are geared towards ensuring that you improve on the quality of your encoded signals before they are stored.

Memory encoding hacks

Memory encoding hacks falls into the following broad categories;

- Attention-focusing hacks
- Chunking hacks

Attention-focusing hacks

The following are some of the common attention-focusing hacks

1. Noise blocking – Noise blocking happens when you use acoustic blockers such as acoustic walls, acoustic ceilings and acoustic windows and doors to block outside noise from entering the audition room (where you want to focus attention to listening). This is commonly applied in recording studios and lecture rooms.

2. Noise filtering – This refers to getting rid of unwanted noise so that attention focuses on wanted piece of audio

signal (information). Noise filtering is done when you have recorded sound and you use electronics filters to get rid of unwanted sound so that what remains is only the wanted sound. Noise filtering can also be done mentally where you deliberately choose to listen to a particular source of sound and ignore the rest. This is commonly applied during meditation or when you are in a noisy environment yet you want to listen to a particular speaker.

3. Focus blinders – Blinders are commonly used in horse races to achieve great results. For example;

- A blinder is put on each side of the eyes of the horse so that the horse doesn't see sideways so that it remains focused on track ahead.

- When it comes to athletics, the race tracks are a form of non-intrusive blinders that directs a runner to focus only on his/her lane so as not to interfere with or obstruct other runners. The same applies to road traffic lines.

- Other places where blinders are placed are cybercafés and audiovisual libraries. Though, most of them are put with the purpose of ensuring privacy, they serve the other purpose of ensuring that whoever is carrying out a certain task is not distracted by unnecessary attention from onlookers. The same concept is also applied to polling booths. If you have shared space and you really want to focus and concentrate, blinders are the best trick for you.

4. Use of cues – A cue is by far one of the most widely applied hacks when it comes to encoding. Though, cues are dual-purpose in the sense that they help in encoding just as they do help in retrieval/recalling. For example;

   - Color Coding – Color coding has been one most widely used encoding techniques in electricity and electronics. When it comes to electrical wiring, the red/brown, blue/black, green/yellow are the three common color codes that denote Live, Neutral and Ground wires, respectively. Color coding is also widely used in electronics when it comes to encoding/decoding details about the Resistor values. This is because a resistor is extremely small, it hard to print sufficient legible characters that can represent its value. Resistors are usually encoded using different orders of the colors of the rainbow with each color having a specific numerical value.

Grey, Brown, Silver, Gold and Black are additional color codes that serves to modify these values (e.g. zero addition, multiplication, powering, positioning, tolerance level, etc)

- Symbolization – Symbolization is a coding and retrieval technique that relies on use of symbols. The most common and widely used symbols are the polarity symbols (+) and (-) denoting positive and negative respectively. Traffic symbols are also widely used.

- Signage – It is hard to distinguish signs and symbols. However, symbols are signs that have much deeper meaning. In this regard, we can consider use of sign language as a way of encoding. For example, when a teacher is teaching elementary mathematics to small kids, he/she will pronounce 'TWO' while raising two fingers as a sign language. This helps to boost encoding and make retrieval easier later on.

- Body language – There is a thin line differentiating between sign language and body language.

However, not all body language is sign language. Some body language can be perceived implicitly without necessarily being expressed through sign language. Another differentiating factor is that sign language is formal while body language is mostly informal. Though there are few commonalities such as nodding, shaking heads, saluting, among others. But, winking, sitting or standing in a certain posture, raising eyebrows, etc. are parts of body language that is not formally recognized as sign language. Furthermore, sign language also falls within the linguistic domain. On the other hand, body language falls within the psychology domain. Using body language can enhance coding of messages into memory.

- Sensory cues – Sensory cues have been widely used in certain scenarios to enforce encoding. They are widely used in training animals, more so dogs and dolphins. In humans, sensory cues are widely used in chemical laboratory training. In this training iconic cues are used in litmus test; olfactory cues are used to encode information about various chemical elements and their distinctions by identifying their particular scent or odor. In Biology, all sensory cues are used for encoding and recall in various ways. For more information on the use of these sensory cues in studies, we shall discuss them in the Section under "Memory Hacks and Strategies to Boost Your Studies".

Chunking hacks

As we saw in our previous section, Chunking is simply the act of grouping similar elements so that they can be encoded together as one unit as opposed to separate units. We saw that short-term memory is highly limited. Most studies suggest that a normal short-term memory can store 5-9 elements/units at a go.

We also understand that nothing can go into the long-term memory without passing through the short-term memory. Thus, how much is stored in the short-term memory at a time will determine how much will be able to be consolidated into the long-term memory.

We understand that not all information is available all the time. For example, a lecture, a product demonstration, a theatre performance, etc. are all time-bound. Unless one records them, then, one will have to device means and ways to capture them as fast and as much as possible. This is where chunking becomes necessary. Furthermore, even if you record them, in certain situations, such as in examination room, you won't be allowed in with your recordings. Thus, you will eventually have to find ways and means of chunking so as to boost your encoding and consolidation.

Examples of Chunking Hacks for Encoding

Chunking applies where you can use a combination of syllables. For example;

If you want to remember 1,9,7,5 you can use a two-syllables chunking or a four syllable chunking

19, 75 is a two-syllable chunking

1975 is a four-syllable chunking

In memory terms, each element has its own bytes of memory allocated to it. There is very minimal variation for each byte. For example, bytes allocated to each of the four digits/elements is not the same but close. A two-digit syllable will occupy much fewer bytes than two separate elements. A four-digit syllable will occupy much fewer bytes than two double-digit syllable and extremely fewer bytes compared each of the four digits/elements.

In memory terms, the four-digit syllable will be lighter to both encode and store as compared to a two-digit syllable and extremely lighter to encode and store compared to four independent digits. The same applies to recalling.

Memory encoding Strategies

1. Boost attention
2. Practice the mentioned memory encoding hacks
3. Continually explore your own hacks that works
4. Cultivate good long-term habits that improves memory

MEMORY CONSOLIDATION AND RETENTION HACKS AND STRATEGIES

As we stated earlier, memory consolidation is the process of converting encoded information from short-term memory into long-term memory. We further noted that consolidation is a continuing process that seeks to remove errors, defragment and optimize long-term memory. This happens every time we recall memory. Whenever we recall a memory, we add new attributes that enhance it and boost its clarity. This is more so when we are revising, editing or even retelling content/story.

Consolidation facilitates retention. We've seen that the brain cleans memory of unwanted content or content that seems no longer useful. The brain evaluates this by determining the frequency by which certain information is retrieved and recalled. The higher the frequency of retrieval, the higher the chances that a certain set of information will not be 'deleted' or gotten rid from the memory. This deletion can be 'temporary' such that what seems not so needed is put into the 'recycle bin' for certain duration. Beyond certain duration, depending on the cost of retention and time passed, it may emptied from the 'recycle bin'. This 'recycle bin' is just but a computer analogy of a part of the long-term memory where information that hardly gets retrieved is consigned to.

Memory consolidation is more about repetition. The more you recall a memory, the more it gets consolidated.

Just like recalling, there are certain hacks that you can use to enhance memory consolidation and retention

Memory consolidation and retention hacks

1. Mnemonics- Mnemonics are used almost all stages and processes of memory, including encoding, consolidation, and recall.

2. Sudoku – Sudoku helps in recalling and consolidation of language vocabularies. It can also be used in consolidation and recalling of facts.

3. Puzzles – puzzles are used in both recalling and consolidation. Crosswords help to build vocabulary and facts. Jigsaw puzzles also serve the same purpose.

Memory consolidation and retention strategies

1. Recite – Reciting is commonly applied in composition, literature, poetry, music, drama, among others. It is more about recalling it as it is, again.

2. Retell – Retell is synonymous with recite. However, it is more appropriate to storytelling. It is more about telling it, again and again. Unlike in reciting, in retelling, you don't have to use exact words, vocals and the like. What matters is that the essence of your story (that is, its subject matter) remains the same. Thus, the words, vocals, style, etc may be different, but, the meaning should remain the same so that those who perceive can relate with the story and feel it is just as the same as it were told previously.

3. Revise – Revising may involve reciting and retelling. But, it is more about going through it again and again. In revising, you can carry out error checking, editing, defragmentation and optimization either physically (as in notes) or mentally (in the memory). When it comes to studying, both physical and mental revising can be applied. We shall see more on this later on under the Section titled "Memory Hacks to Boost Your Studies".

4. Practice consolidation using the mentioned memory consolidation and retention hacks.

5. Explore your own memory consolidation and retention hacks that work.

6. Cultivate good long-term habits that improves your memory.

MEMORY RECALL HACKS AND STRATEGIES

Memory recall and retrieval is by far the most significant part of our memory process. Of course encoding, consolidation and storage are important. But, of what use will stored memory be if it can't be recalled? It is almost of no worth.

Thus, though encoding is a challenge, the greatest challenge is that of recalling. Nonetheless, we cannot overlook encoding as you cannot recall that which was not encoded and thereafter stored. It goes without saying that how information is encoded (and cued) will heavily contribute to how easy it will be recalled. Thus, encoding cannot be overlooked. We shall discuss memory encoding under Hacks in the subsequent sections.

Memory recall is a significant part of memory improvement strategies. Thus, we need to have a good understanding of it to be able to device appropriate strategies.

Types of memory recall

There are three basic types of memory recall;

1. Free recall
2. Serial recall

3. Cued recall

Free recall

This is recalling items in any order. The order in which items occurred is immaterial.

Serial recall

This is recalling events in the order in which they occurred. The order is extrememly important. This is so when it comes to recalling episodic memory.

Cued recall

This occurs when events are recalled based on a certain trigger or cue.

Memory recall hacks

The following are great memory recall hacks;

Mnemonics – A mnemonic is a device or technique that helps you to recall information. Common examples of mnemonics include acronyms, rhymes, phrases, image maps, among others. For example "**R**ichard **O**f **Y**ork **G**ave **B**irth **I**n **V**ain" is a mnemonic phrase that helps you to remember the order of colors of a rainbow. The first letter of each word represents a rainbow color. E.g. 'R' for red, 'O' for orange, 'Y' for Yellow, 'G' for green, 'B' for blue, 'I' for indigo and 'V' for violet.

Memory cues – All the memory cues we discussed under encoding memory are the same ones that are used to recall. You can't use a cue to encode a memory if you won't need to use it to recall the same memory. For example, you can't use a bookmark or index tag in a library to store information about a particular book or page if you have no intention of using the very same bookmark or index tag for retrieval. If you do so, then, you are overloading your memory for no reason. It will be a waste of time and energy.

Mantras – Mantras are commonly used to aid recitation

Mala – Mala beads are commonly used in recalling things. Each bead represents a certain set of information.

Memory recall strategies

1. Practice recalling using the mentioned memory recall hacks

2. Create conducive environment for recalling – recalling can be impaired by noise or other distraction. This is the main reason as to why silence and removal of unnecessary distractions are always demanded in an exam room.

3. Cultivate good long-term habits that improves your memory

MEMORY HACKS TO BOOST YOUR STUDIES

The most important application where your memory is always tested to the limits is while studying for exams. When you are a student, this becomes inevitable.

Luckily, studying seems to have the giant share of all possible memory hacks. This is probably because learning transcends all environments, whether you are a student or worker, in a classroom or kitchen, wherever you are, learning opportunities keep on bombarding you.

Memory hacks to boost your studies

The following are memory hacks to boost your studies;

1. Use mnemonics
2. Use chunking
3. Use puzzles
    - Sudoku

- Crosswords
- Jigsaw
- etc

4. Use visualization tools to present your data – tables, graphs, pie charts, tree diagrams, network diagrams, decomposition charts, histograms, etc, are among the best visualization tools that you can use to visualize your data/content. There are modern tools and apps available that can help you make complex visualizations of extra-ordinary data such as Big data.

Memory strategies to boost your studies

1. Create your own puzzles. It is easier to acquire ready-made puzzles. However, they may not necessarily meet your specific study needs. The best way to meet your specific study needs is to create your own puzzles. You can do this with your study-mates. Creating itself reinforces your memory.

2. Actively revise. Revise is much more than re-reading. It is about going through the content not only to remind yourself but discover new perspectives, new dimensions and new ways of presenting facts and information.

3. Recite – Yes, this is not only for poetry. Even then, you can turn every piece of your study content into poems. Nonetheless, to recite is not just by use of your vocals, but also use of your pen (writing); use of your hands (re-creating), among others.

4. Retell – The best way to remember history is to narrate it. This enhances your episodic memory. It is not just history that you can retell. You can retell virtually every other subject. Yes, you can retell how your lecturer showed a certain mathematical example; drew a certain chemical bond; made a certain physics experiment; and so on and so forth. Just repackage the information into a retellable form.

5. Try different ways of presentation so as to utilize as many of your sensory memory as possible. Visualization is so powerful as it applies to all kinds of studies. Use tables, graphs, tree diagrams, network paths, decomposition charts, etc, so as to present your study content.

MEMORY HACKS TO BOOST YOUR WORK

Apart from studying environment, work environment is the other environment that occupies most of our time and demands so much of our memory. This is more the case if your profession is so technical such that you have to keep on referring to learning materials just to update yourself and remain relevant to the demands of your service.

Work, more so, routine work requires you to boost your implicit memory so that you don't stress up your working memory to recall things that would rather be done elsewhere. Your working memory should be for those tasks that require active creativity at all times. Routine work should be consigned to implicit/unconscious memory where they will be called upon as the situation demands.

No office lacks routine activities. You have to identify those routine activities, find the best procedures required to execute them in the most efficient and effective ways. Once you identify the procedures, master them through practice, among other hacks and strategies so that they stick in your implicit memory. This way, your working memory won't be overworked and your brain won't be stressed. You can also look at automating them if possible. This will allow you to focus more on creative activities.

Memory hacks to boost your work

Every work environment is unique. This means that each work environment has its own unique hacks. For example, those hacks that are uniquely particular to an office typist won't probably apply to a garage mechanic. Nonetheless, the following are general universal hacks that can apply in every work environment;

1. Punctuality hacks – Always have an alarm clock to remind you what to do at certain specific times e.g. waking up, walking out to work, breaking for lunch, leaving work, going for gym, preparing dinner, etc.

2. Procedural routine hacks – A mnemonic clock (also referred to as 'talking' clock) which you can program to talk to you what to do next when you are executing a certain procedural task

3. Events hacks – Use diary and calendars to reminding you on what to do during certain days.

4. Task to do hacks – have a 'To Do' list of task you are expected to perform during a given day. This will ensure that you don't forget or inadvertently skip an important task

5. Journalizing hacks – Journals are a great way to enhance episodic memory. After attending an event, write down what happened in a detailed summary into your journal. If possible, attach photos of events or quite their references in the album.

6. Recording hacks - Equip yourself with recording tools. Where possible, make recordings of demos, trainings, seminars, etc. Your employer may organize live recording of some important events but not all. If there are certain events that you feel you ought to record, do so. But, seek permission from your supervisor so as not to infringe on any policy or your intention gets misconstrued.

Memory strategies to boost your work

1. Cultivate routine habits - Without routine habits you can hardly implement the mentioned hacks. For example, without cultivating a habit of recording things into your diary, calendar, journal, To Do list, etc, you will hardly have anything to refer to, and even if there is something,

there will be lack of consistency. Recording boosts your memory.

2. Be disciplined – Routines break due to indiscipline. For example, it is common to set an alarm to wake up in the morning. Yet, every time it rings, you snooze it or even switch it off. Every time you do this, you weaken your willpower and in the process create a counter-routine or counter-habit.

3. Be creative – Keep learning new ways of doing the same things. Even if it is a routine, change how you approach it. This will boost the distinctiveness which increases the chances of memorization. Yes, changing the melody or sound of an alarm can wake you up even when you would have otherwise snoozed it or switched it off. The surprise alerts your brain.

4. Cultivate good long-term habits that improves your memory

MEMORY HACKS TO BOOST YOUR HOME ACTIVITIES

When you are not in class or office, or any other place, you are most likely at home. Home is where you retire to. It is where you go to rest and be with your family and loved ones. Thus, it is important to optimize the value you gain or impart through your time spent and activities done while at home.

Some of the things that you are likely going to forget are;

- Shopping for cooking ingredients
- Closing the tap
- Removing food when ready and witching off the cooker
- Carrying your packed food to work or school
- Feeding your pet
- Washing soaked clothes
- Changing your kids nappies
- Forgetting to watch your favorite TV program

Memory hacks to boost your home activities

To address the indicated activities that you are likely going to forget, the following are some of the hacks that you can implement;

1. Prepare a To Do List – Have a To Do list of all the tasks you ought to do the next day. Review and update the list in the morning. Implement the list step by step.

2. Use highlighter labels – Highlighter labels are so far the best approach to remind you of things such as shopping for cooking ingredients, washing soaked clothes, etc. Use labels of different colors to highlight the most important things to do. For example, changing kid's nappies can be highlighted by writing that on a Red label. Feeding your pet can be highlighted by writing that on a Yellow label. Washing your soaked clothes can be highlighted by writing that on a Blue label. The colors show the order of importance. Put your labels in the most conspicuous place. For example, the place you look at first when you open your main door to enter.

3. Use alarm – You can also use an alarm to remind you of almost all of these activities. However, this can only be possible if you are certainly sure of the timings and

your arrival to the house. Also, it depends on the memory capacity your alarm clock in terms of how many alarms you can set and how much descriptions per alarm you can give.

4. Use TV program timer – For TV, every remote control has a timer that prompts the TV to give a beeping sound (some kind of alarm) just to alert you that your preferred program is about to start. Furthermore, some Smart TVs have provisions that allows you to set programs so that they automatically switch to relevant programs based to your schedule.

Memory strategies to boost your home activity

Just like work strategies, you need to:

1. Cultivate routine habits

2. Be disciplined

3. Be creative

4. Cultivate good long-term habits that improves your memory

In addition:

1. Let your family members too be your reminders. In doing so, they also practice on improving their very own memory. That way, it becomes a whole family memory improvement affair.

MEMORY HACKS TO BOOST YOUR RELATIONSHIPS

Relationships and memories are conjoined twins. You cannot develop relationship with people when you can't remember their identity or remember the moments of your interactions with them.

Relationship is built over time by encoding and retaining perceptions of stimuli and signals received from the other party over time. It is the consolidation of these perceptions through repetitive cycles of encoding-storage-recall that determines the depth of a relationship. It brings forth recognition, understanding, acceptance and eventually strengthening of mutual bonds.

For example, if you utter to someone "I love you", it is bound to surprise and raise anxiety, irrespective of whether the reaction will be positive or not. However, if the same is not going to be repeated or expressed through action to enforce it, it is bound fade away from memory over time. It will naturally die off from the memory. Thus, it is repetitions through words and deeds that will reinforce it into the memory through consolidation and eventually result into positive outcome – love and romance.

On the other hand, just saying "I love you" by word of mouth alone, that is using auditory cues alone, it will eventually fail the distinctiveness test and thus become as ordinary as any other word. Thus, for relationship to thrive, you will need to reinforce it with other forms of sensory cues such as olfactory cues, gustatory cues, iconic cues and hepatic cues. It is how you optimize these sensory cues that will boost romance and maximize the impact.

Of course, feedback from the other party is very important. The feedback is the control trigger that should advice you what cues to retreat and which ones to enhance.

This is just one of the scenarios. Relationships are quite wide and diverse and involves different parties including that between siblings, between parents and their children, between supervisors and their juniors, between peers, between neighbors, etc. There none of these relationships where memory is less required.

Memory hacks to boost your relationship

1. Always use a person's names when greeting and bidding farewell. This is an auditory cue that helps you to remember names of people in your relationships and also boosts your auditory or echoic memory.

2. Always try to implicitly but subtly replicate or mimic the other person's important cues. This helps in the process of encoding

3. Make effort of maintaining eye contact to enhance iconic memory.

4. Make effort of using touch cues such as handshakes, hugs or kisses (where appropriate) when meeting and also when parting ways. Each of them is unique no matter the number of repetitions. This way, you are able to enhance hepatic memory through encoding and consolidation.

5. Kisses (where appropriate), when used, helps to enhance gustatory memory. Use them often if you are in a romantic relationship.

6. Women are great at using the power of olfactory cues. They are also sensitive to smell, especially men's sweat scent. The challenge is for men to emulate them and properly employ olfactory cues. This enhances olfactory memory.

7. To further enhance auditory cues (to which women are good recipients) take advantage of your vocals to pronounce certain keywords that you believe that can trigger the right response on the other party. This is not

just for personal relationships but also works well in other relationships such as business relationship.

8. To further enhance iconic cues (to which men are good recipients), accentuate your looks. Hairdo, nail polish, a label on lapel, subtle lip balm, treated eyebrows and eyelashes, meticulous dressing, among others, are some of the things you can do to accentuate your looks. All these are potential cues. You never know which of them will create a lasting memory in the other party that you are engaging. This too transcends all forms of relationships, be they formal or informal. You only got to observe the boundaries of each.

Memory strategies to boost your relationships

1. Use the power of your sensory cues. Neurolinguistic Programming (NLP) has great techniques that can help you succeed in boosting the power of your sensory cues.

2. Practice, practice! A one-off attempt soon fades. Keep improving on your cues. Keep changing them if you are dealing with one party. Yes, obey the power of **distinctiveness**.

3. Cultivate good long-term habits that improve your memory.

AGE-RELATED MEMORY HACKS AND STRATEGIES

Ageing is a normal process of life. All faculties of your life are affected as your body increasingly become frail. Your brain and memory are not spared. You experience natural memory loss as you age.

However, just as you can slow down the pace of ageing by engineering positive lifestyle changes, you too can slow down the pace of memory loss through hacks and strategies.

Age-related memory hacks

1. Keep a routine

2. Keep things organized and orderly – Put things always in the same place

3. Organize your information in a systematic manner – Put things in a diary or day planner

4. Involve your senses – Find ways to use sensory cues

5. Make associations – Attach new information to things that you already know

6. Repeat information that you are prone to forgetting – For example, make a habit of repeating names of new people that you meet

7. Make a quick run through the alphabet if there is a vocabulary that you've forgot – The right alphabetical letter will serve as a verbal cue that will trigger your memory recall.

8. Tell stories – When you tell a story about an event, you boost your very own episodic memory through the process of consolidation. In traditional societies such as in Asia and Africa where storytelling was normal daily routine by the elderly, their episodic memory is highly vivid.

9. Teach others – Like telling stories, teaching others boosts the process of consolidation.

10. Get enough rest and full night sleep to boost consolidation

Age-related memory strategies

As we have seen, aging is a normal process that affects all your faculties of life including your studies, work, home activities and relationships, among others. It also affects all stages of processes of your memory including encoding, consolidation, storage/retention, and recall/retrieval. Thus, all previously mention strategies do apply.

However, it is important to mention that beyond youth-hood, as you get older, the more critical the mobility exercises and fitness workouts become. Furthermore, the impact of High-Intensity Interval Training (HIIT) on your brain and memory improvement becomes more pronounced. HIIT is a kind of fitness workout characterized by intervals of sudden bursts of vigorous exercises (high intensity) interspersed with intervals of low intensity workouts. For example, you can have sprinting intervals interspersed with jogging intervals. Just to re-emphasize, mobility exercises must be given priority as they boost blood circulation in the brain which ensures adequate oxygen supply, among other critical resources.

LONG-TERM LIFESTYLE HABITS TO IMPROVE YOUR MEMORY

While there are hacks to improve your memory, they must be complemented by long-term lifestyle habits for you to achieve a wholesome lasting outcome.

The following are long-term lifestyle habits that you need to engender;

1. Good dietary habits
2. Mobility exercise and fitness habits
3. Leisure habits
4. Rest habits
5. Learn and keep learning
6. Have enough sleep
7. Psychological habits

Dietary habits

Diet has direct impact on your memory. Like any other part of your body, your brain needs energy to function. It also needs proteins to rebuild and repair itself. It needs essential minerals for various chemical activities including encoding, storage and retrieval.

There are certain diets that are known to boost your brain function, more so, your memory. However, focusing so much on them can be detrimental to other body organs and needs. Thus, the best strategy is to take wholesome quality balanced diet.

The following are dietary habits that you need to engender;

- Have balanced diet – This should include carbohydrates, proteins, vitamins and essential fatty acids. Make sure that your food has sufficient fiber.

- Practice clean eating – This is eating food as close to natural as possible.

- Avoid trans-fats – Trans-fats are those fats which get highly hydrogenated when applied excess heat such as during frying. Instead of trans-fats, use olive oil and coconut oil.

- Avoid bad sugar – More so, eat foods that contain natural sugar rather than those that requires you to add table sugar. Give preference to fibrous carbohydrates. Refined carbohydrates create rapid surges in your blood sugar level which has negative effect on your brain and memory.

Mobility exercises and fitness habits

Mobile exercises and fitness habits – studies have shown that mobile exercises and fitness habits have a profound influence on your memory, more so, as you age. The older you become the more profound is the impact. The emphasis is on mobility exercises.

Leisure habits

Leisure helps to unwind your mind by switching off from normal routine to more distinct activities. Furthermore, doing things that you love doing, as opposed to those you have to do, triggers the 'feel good' hormones which brings forth laughter, smiles, sharing of jokes, affectionate touches, among other things. All these have been found out to greatly boost your memory.

To optimize your leisure habits for greater memory improvement, try to engage in new distinct activities each and every other time.

Rest habits

Due to busy study and work schedules, people hardly find time to rest. However, there is simply nothing like 'lack of time'. Everyone has 24 hours a day, 7 days a week and 365/366 days a year. There is no one who has more time than the other. So, it is all about prioritization. If you consider your rest as not a priority compared to other engagements, you "won't have time" for it.

Inadequate rest is one of the greatest thieves of working memory. If you don't have sufficient rest; focus, concentration and attention will be low. This will impair your memory encoding and consolidation. It will also impair your memory recall and retrieval.

Have more definite rest schedule. This helps to tune your mind and helps your brain and the rest of body prepare itself.

Have enough sleep

Like rest, sleeping is very important. In fact, studies have proven that a sleep before and after heavy memory engaging activity such as studying helps to boost memory consolidation. While you are asleep your memory is refreshing, repairing, defragmenting and optimizing itself. This is one of the reasons that you have dreams when you are deeply asleep. It is like a memory reel being run over the projector which cast images on your mind which turns out in form of dreams.

Psychological habits

There are several psychological habits that you need to sharpen in order to boost your memory. These include;

- Meditation – Do meditate often. Research has shown that meditation not only boosts consolidation but also recall.

- Self-esteem – Build your self-esteem. This helps you to avoid focusing on recalling negative memories. These are probably the only memories you need to mute or get rid of. But before you succeed, don't trigger them through worries, regrets, jealousy, grudges and such like other things that only reinforce the negative memory through consolidation. These are signs of negative self-image. Instead, focus on the positive side of your memory by using cues that enable you to remember them. Scheduling to call a loving friend, listening to inspirational music and speeches, reading inspirational or motivational stories and going out for leisure are some of the activities that help to boost positive self-esteem.

Learn and keep learning

Keep on learning so as to discover new hacks, strategies and long-term lifestyle habits to improve your memory. You will be a winner!

CONCLUSION

Thank you for acquiring this book and reading it all the way through.

It is my sincere hope that you have gained valuable lessons and gotten inspired to improve your memory – through proven practical memory improvement hacks and strategies.

It is also my sincere hope that you have been able to share knowledge and information gathered from this book with others, and more so, memory hacks and strategies, so that they too can enjoy the benefits improved mental acuity and productive life. Please, do encourage them to have this book as a point of reference for their everyday memory improvement practices.

Again, thank for acquiring this book!

Good luck.

www.ingramcontent.com/pod-product-compliance
Lightning Source LLC
Chambersburg PA
CBHW071009080526
44587CB00015B/2400